ASTROLOGY

LEO

BY ABBY DOTY

Apex is distributed by North Star Editions:
sales@northstareditions.com | 888-417-0195

Produced for Apex by Red Line Editorial.

Photographs ©: Shutterstock Images, cover (illustration, constellation), cover (background), 4–5, 6, 8, 9, 10–11, 12–13, 14–15, 16–17, 18–19, 21, 22–23, 24–25, 26, 29; iStockphoto, 1, 7; SDO/GSFC/NASA, 20

Library of Congress Control Number: 2025939152

ISBN
979-8-89250-785-1 (hardcover)
979-8-89250-814-8 (paperback)
979-8-89250-871-1 (ebook pdf)
979-8-89250-843-8 (hosted ebook)

Printed in the United States of America
Mankato, MN
012026

NOTE TO PARENTS AND EDUCATORS

Apex books are designed to build literacy skills in striving readers. Exciting, high-interest content attracts and holds readers' attention. The text is carefully leveled to allow students to achieve success quickly. Additional features, such as bolded glossary words for difficult terms, help build comprehension.

TABLE OF CONTENTS

CHAPTER 1

THE LION

Leo is a **constellation**. It has nine main stars. People say they look like a lion. *Leo* means "lion" in Latin.

Some of Leo's stars form a hook shape. That part is the lion's head.

Mesopotamia is an area in southwest Asia. Some of the world's oldest kingdoms began there.

A Greek **astronomer** wrote about Leo in the 100s CE. But people studied the constellation long before that. People in Mesopotamia were one example.

STRONG SKIN

The ancient Greeks linked Leo with a **myth** about the Nemean lion. This monster attacked people. It had tough skin. No weapons could hurt it. But the hero Heracles fought and killed it.

Heracles grabbed the Nemean lion and choked it.

Ancient Egyptians had a similar constellation. It was seen as important. The sun seemed to move near it in the summer. The Nile River flooded at that time. The water helped plants grow.

The sun was an important part of religion in ancient Egypt.

Regulus is one of the brightest stars in the sky. It's part of the lion's chest.

FAST FACT

Leo is one of the oldest constellations.

CHAPTER 2

SUMMER SIGN

Leo is one of the 12 **zodiac** signs. These signs are used in astrology. They are said to shape people's lives and **personalities**.

Some people use zodiac signs as a way to look for patterns in how people think or feel.

Each sign is matched with a constellation and a part of the year. Leo is the fifth sign. Its season begins around July 23. It ends around August 22.

The zodiac constellations are part of the ecliptic. That's the path the sun seems to follow in the sky as Earth moves around it.

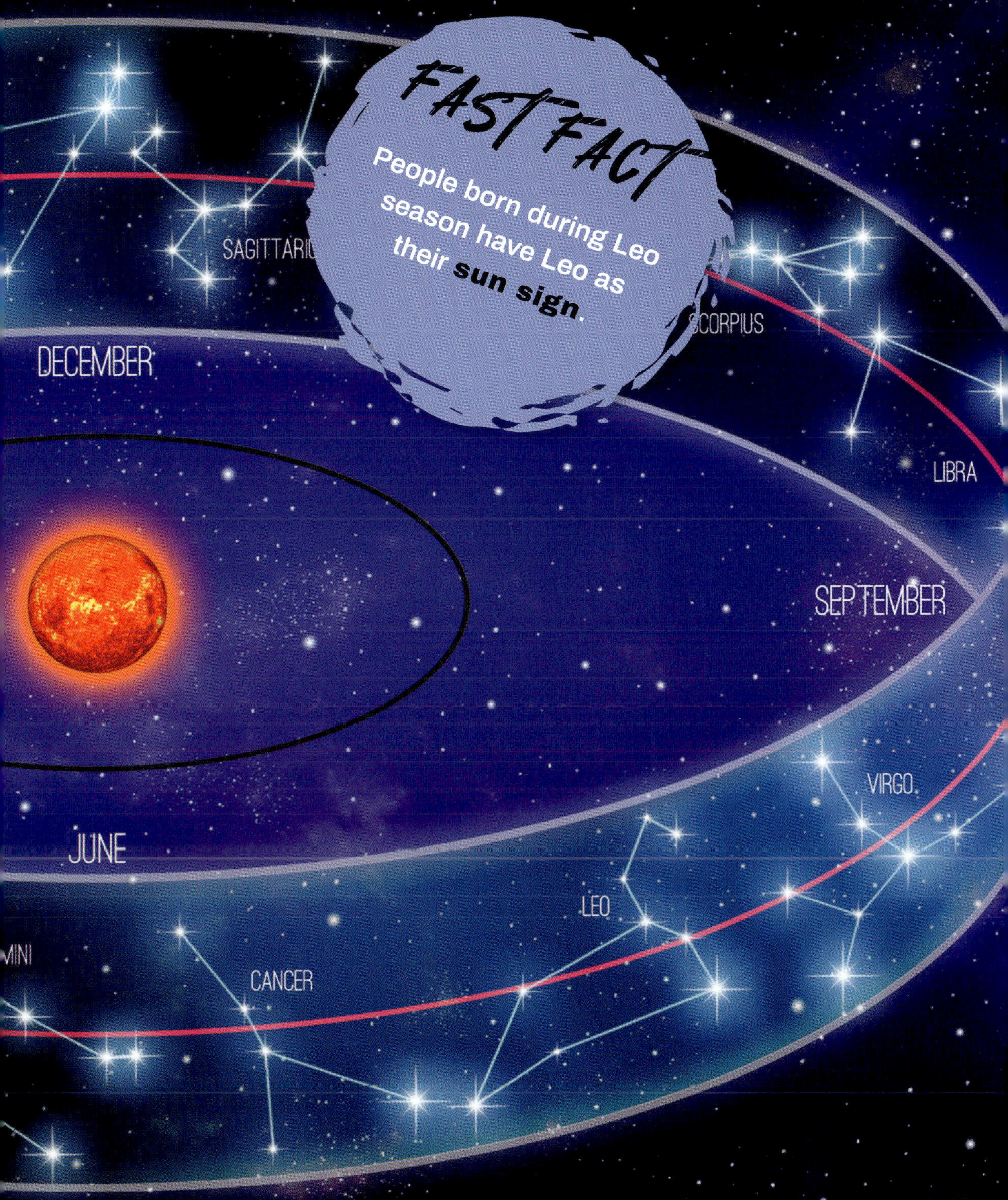

FAST FACT

People born during Leo season have Leo as their **sun sign**.

In northern parts of the world, Leo season is in the summer. Summer is a time of warmth and light. And Leos are said to have big hearts and bright personalities.

LEO SEASON

In astrology, Leos are known for being brave and bold. During Leo season, other signs may take on these traits. People may be more confident. They may take risks or try new things.

Like summer, Leo season can be a time of joy and adventure.

CHAPTER 3

ABOUT LEO

Every zodiac sign has a **glyph**. Leo's is a small circle with a squiggly line coming out of it. This shape represents a lion.

The curvy line in Leo's glyph looks kind of like a lion's mane or tail.

Each sign has an element, too. Leo's element is fire. As a result, Leos can be both warm and **dramatic**.

Each element is named after a different part of nature.

ELEMENTS

The zodiac uses four elements. They are air, earth, fire, and water. Three signs go with each element. Those signs often share traits. For example, fire signs all have lots of energy.

The sun is the center of the solar system.

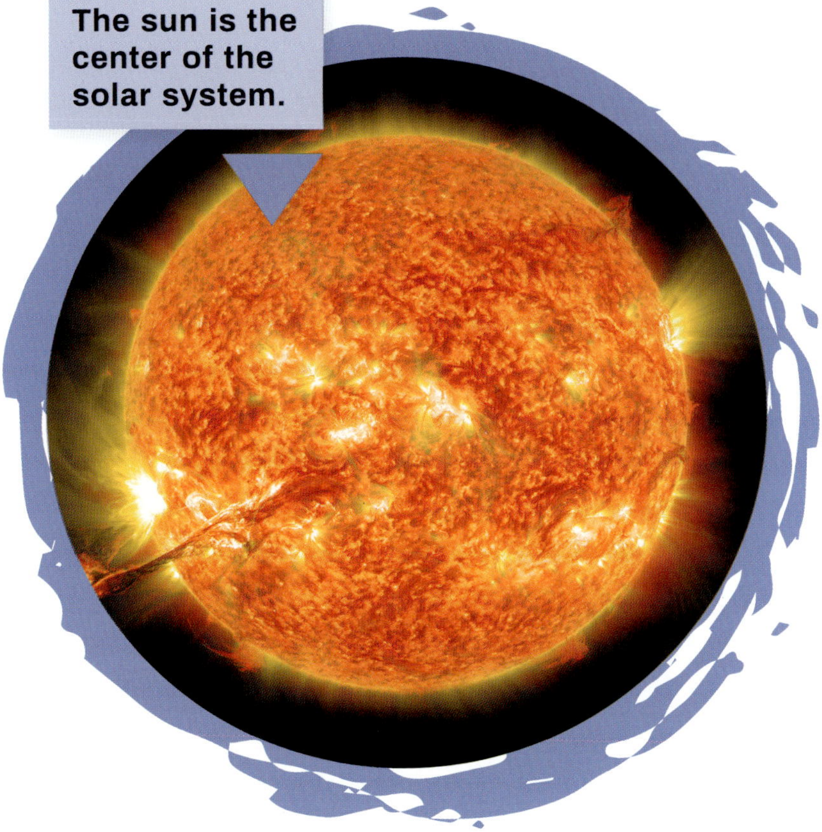

Most signs have ruling planets that are said to shape how they act. But Leo is ruled by the sun. Like the sun, Leos tend to draw others in.

FAST FACT

Sunlight helps things grow. And Leos often help others.

Leos tend to speak, act, and dress in ways that other people like and want to copy.

CHAPTER 4

LEO LEADERS

In astrology, Leos are described as leaders. They often have lots of friends. And many Leos are good at talking with people.

Many Leos are great at helping others have fun and feel welcome.

Many Leos enjoy creating and performing. They may get jobs in fashion or acting. Leos aren't afraid to express their ideas. And they work hard to reach their goals.

FAST FACT

Famous Leos include Tom Brady, Charli XCX, and Jason Momoa.

Charli XCX is known for her hit songs and bold choices.

Many Leos love being the center of attention. But many also enjoy helping others follow their dreams. Leos protect others, too. They will stand up to make sure people are treated fairly.

SHARE THE SPOTLIGHT

Some Leos feel upset when other people get attention. They may act out to get it back. But Leos can learn to share the spotlight.

Leos tend to be kind, loyal friends.

COMPREHENSION QUESTIONS

Write your answers on a separate piece of paper.

1. Write a few sentences explaining the main ideas of Chapter 3.
2. Do you like being a leader? Why or why not?
3. What is Leo's element?
   - **A.** water
   - **B.** air
   - **C.** fire
4. According to astrology, which job might a Leo enjoy?
   - **A.** being the head of a big company
   - **B.** working alone in a quiet library
   - **C.** working from home on a computer

5. What does **traits** mean in this book?

In astrology, Leos are known for being brave and bold. During Leo season, other signs may take on these ***traits****.*

A. types of animals
B. ways of acting
C. times of day

6. What does **protect** mean in this book?

Leos ***protect*** *others, too. They will stand up to make sure people are treated fairly.*

A. cover up
B. help out
C. chase away

Answer key on page 32.

GLOSSARY

astronomer
A person who studies objects in space.

confident
Feeling sure of yourself.

constellation
A group of stars that form a shape.

dramatic
Tending to act in ways that show big feelings.

glyph
A shape that stands for a word or idea.

myth
A well-known story from the past that often includes magic.

personalities
The ways that people usually act.

sun sign
Someone's main zodiac sign, said to shape their core traits.

zodiac
The set of 12 signs used in astrology, based on a part of the sky that the sun appears to move through each year.

TO LEARN MORE

BOOKS

Betts, Bruce. *The Sun: Our Solar System's Star*. Lerner Publications, 2025.

Goldstein, Margaret J. *Mysteries of Stars*. Lerner Publications, 2021.

Loh-Hagan, Virginia. *Star Signs*. Cherry Lake Publishing, 2021.

ONLINE RESOURCES

Visit **www.apexeditions.com** to find links and resources related to this title.

ABOUT THE AUTHOR

Abby Doty is a writer, editor, and booklover from Minnesota. Her sun sign is Aquarius.

INDEX

ANSWER KEY:
1. Answers will vary; 2. Answers will vary; 3. C; 4. A; 5. B; 6. B